Robert Graham

New York City and its Masters

Robert Graham

New York City and its Masters

ISBN/EAN: 9783337415808

Printed in Europe, USA, Canada, Australia, Japan

Cover: Foto ©Andreas Hilbeck / pixelio.de

More available books at **www.hansebooks.com**

AND

ITS MASTERS.

BY

ROBERT GRAHAM,

GENERAL SECRETARY OF THE CHURCH TEMPERANCE SOCIETY

———————

NEW YORK:

CHURCH TEMPERANCE SOCIETY'S OFFICES,

ANNEX HALL, 16 FOURTH AVENUE.

—

1887.

TO THE MAN

WHO HAS TAKEN THE TRUEST MEASURE

OF THE LIQUOR TRAFFIC OF THE CITY OF NEW YORK ٭

AND HAS BEEN THE MOST ACTIVE AND PERSISTENT ADVOCATE

FOR ITS RESTRICTION,

THE REV. HOWARD CROSBY, D.D.

I RESPECTFULLY INSCRIBE THIS

PAMPHLET.

.

ROBERT GRAHAM.

NEW YORK, Feb. 1st, 1887.

NEW YORK CITY AND ITS MASTERS.

OUR POSITION.

THE three main objects of the Church Temperance Society are:

1. The promotion of Temperance.
2. The rescue of the Intemperate.
3. The removal of the causes of Intemperance.

It does not denounce the temperate use of intoxicating liquors as a sin. Whilst it believes in increasing the resisting power of the individual by moral and religious agencies, it recognizes to its fullest extent the dangers arising from extreme and indiscriminate licensing of saloons, and aims at the dimunition of the temptation.

It is non-political and has no party affiliations.

Believing that the first step toward the cure of the disease is a full diagnosis of the case, it has at some cost and labor endeavored to fairly and dispassionately state the deep ramifications of the liquor traffic in New York, in the hope that the Empire City which has offered a home to men of all Nationalities, will ultimately choose for its rulers the best and not the worst, and that one of the first steps to be taken to that end will be to dethrone the saloon from its position of political supremacy, and to relegate its owners to a back seat.

I.

NEW YORK CITY POPULATION.

· NOTHING in the world's history shows so marvellous an increase of population as the United States of America during the past thirty years.

In 1850 its population was			23,191,816.
In 1860 "	"	"	31,443,321.
In 1870 "	"	"	38,558,371.
In 1880 "	"	"	50,155,783.

This enormous growth has not been by the law of natural increase, but by a constantly growing foreign immigration of · which the largest factors are the Irish and the German.

Side by side with this general expansion has been the marked trend of population to large cities. In 1850 the number of cities was 85 ; in 1860, 141 ; in 1870, 225, and 1880, 286. The proportion of the city to the general population has necessarily undergone a marked change. In 1850 it was 12.5 per cent. ; in 1860, 16.1 ; in 1870, 20.9 and in 1880, 22.5.

The State of New-York with an aggregate population of 5,082,862, of which 3,871,492 is native, and 1,211,370 foreign born, contains 12 cities of more than 20,000 population : viz :

New York	1,206,299
Brooklyn	566,663
Buffalo	155,134
Albany	90,758
Rochester	89,366
Troy	56,747
Syracuse	51,792
Utica	33,914
Auburn	21,924
Oswego	21,116
Elmira	20,541
Poughkeepsie	20,247

Total 2,334,501

or a proportion of 46 per cent.

New York City, from its position as the great port of entry, naturally receives more than its due proportion of foreign emigrants, and also in more liberal measure than is fully appreciated by "those who have left their country for their country's good." Of its population of 1,206,299, 727,629 are native and 478,670 foreign born. Leaving out of present consideration the large number of those who are of foreign descent, one generation removed, and whose affinities are still strongly to their native land, the distinctively foreign born population of New York City comprises the following nationalities :

Irish	198,595
German	163,482
English and Welsh	30,593
Italian	12,223
Polish	9,029
French	9,910
Bohemian	8,093
Scotch	8,083
British American	7,004
Austrian	4,743
Russian	4,551
Swiss	4,545
Hungarian	4,101
Swedish	4,087

This extraordinary conjunction of nationalities—the fact that in certain parts of the city their boundaries are sharply defined —that you can put your finger on the Italian quarter, the Bohemian quarter—that there is still an Irish vote and a German vote—that these nationalties are slowly fusing and blending in the crucible of national life, with the scum still at the top and the dregs at the bottom, makes social, legislative and religious questions intricate and difficult of solution.

II.

SALOONS VERSUS CHURCHES AND SCHOOLS.

SALOONS.

I WILL not soon forget my first look at New York City six years ago ; its grand expansive bay, the wooded heights of Staten and Long Island left and right ; the junction of the two great rivers which wash the shores of Manhattan Island and mark it out at no distant day as the great commercial center of the world ; and in front the long, narrow ridge crowned island, which within living memory has drawn to itself so vast and dense a population.

For criminal and police purposes the city is divided into thirty-five police precincts, and for purposes of State Legislation into twenty-four Assembly Districts.

As Legislation is an important factor in dealing with the liquor traffic, I have selected the area of the Assembly Districts, rather than that of police precincts or ·wards, because I hope to prove how enormous and direct is the influence of the saloon on the nomination and vote of our Assembly and Senate, and therefore how largely increased is the difficulty of passing any restrict-ive enactments tending to limit the growth, or diminish the profit of a trade which has its hands on the throttle valve of the legislative engine.

By the courtesy of the present Board of Excise Commission-ers, I was given the fullest access to the books of the depart-ment, and through the Society's agent had a complete list made of all the liquor licenses granted during the year ending April 30th, 1886 ; together with the location of the saloon, the name of the keeper, and as far as could be ascertained, his nation-ality. There are two great educational agencies directly hostile to each other, viz : The Saloon v. Church and School.

From the books of the Excise Commissioners, as above stated, I have obtained the following carefully verified statement of

Licenses granted year ending April 30th, 1886.

1st Grade.—Hotel....................	License fee $250.00....	17
2nd " "	" 100.00....	80
3rd " Saloon....................	" 75.00....	8,055
4th " Storekeeper (sale off)....	" 75.00....	518
5th " Saloon (Beer only)......	" 30.00....	904

Total Licenses granted.......... 9,574
Number lapsed or revoked during the year.......... 406

Number now in existence.......... 9,168
Estimated number of places selling without license, disreputable and gambling houses where liquor is sold....... 1,000

Total number of places where liquor is obtained....10,168

Estimating the increase of population since the census of 1880 as now reaching 1,400,000, we have roughly a liquor saloon for every 140 of the population, including men, women and children. The following are number and class of

LICENSED SALOONS IN POLICE PRECINCTS (1885–6).

Police Precincts.	Class 1.	Class 2.	Class 3.	Class 4.	Class 5.	Total Licenses Granted.	Lapsed or Revoked.	Licenses Now Expiring.	Police Precincts.
1	3	3	266	42	1	315	3	312	1
2	"	"	257	"	5	34	4	30	2
3	"	"	"	"	"	"	"	"	3
4	"	2	315	7	21	345	1	344	4
5	"	2	248	13	8	271	"	271	5
6	. "	4	227	7	9	247	"	247	6
7	"	"	175	1	28	204	"	204	7
8	"	1	290	6	19	316	2	314	8
9	"	1	301	14	14	330	8	322	9
10	"	3	481	7	100	591	3	588	10
11	"	"	299	7	65	371	"	371	11
12	"	"	283	27	27	337	1	336	12
13	"	1	232	2	56	291	19	.272	13
14	1	2	240	12	42	279	18	261	14
15	2	9	233	21	10	275	17	258	15
16	"	1	216	18	12	247	15	232	16
17	1	1	545	20	80	647	49	598	17
18	"	8	317	18	28	371	19	352	18
19	1	5	331	31	23	391	21	370	19
20	"	"	476	11	25	512	35	477	20
21	1	"	295	24	29	349	30	319	21
22	"	4	469	38	16	527	27	500	22
23	" .	1	376	34	22	433	21	412	23
24									24
25									25
26									26
27	1	4	343	38	38	424	37	387	27
28	"	2	357	33	22	417	37	377	28
29	11	267	288	47	15	388	22	366	29
30	"	2	95	16	22	135	10	125	30
31	"	1	80	14	15	110	2	108	31
32	"	"	31	2	26	59	1	58	32
33	"	"	197	6	59	262	3	259	33
34	"	"	53	2	28	83	1	82	34
35	"	1	26	1	17	45	"	45	35
	21	85	8,114	519	844	9,603	406	9,197	

It is an undoubted fact that just where the poverty and misery is greatest there is the largest number of saloons.

Granted squalid and overcrowded homes, with a minimum of comfort and a maximum of filth, it is not to be wondered at that saloons with polished woods, meretricious gilding, light, warmth and freedom should compete with and beat out of the field the three bare and comfortless rooms which are home only in name.

To the real home in the city of New York, which is within the reach of every man in it, there can be no deadlier enemy than the 10,168 saloons which crowd its alleys and throng its courts.

12

CHURCHES AND PUBLIC SCHOOLS.

IT is a fact painfully true that as wealth and competence moves up town, churches move with it. Draw a line across the city at Eighth Street from North to East River and you will have emphasized the fact that from that line to the Battery churches are "conspicuous by their absence," and the saloon is the dominant factor in molding social, political and religious life. New-York is generous in its educational appliances. Teachers, buildings and apparatus are all on a liberal scale : and yet note the following list of religious and educational centers of good :

DENOMINATIONS.	CHURCHES.	CHAPELS.	TOTAL.
Protestant Episcopal	73	9	82
Roman Catholic	61	"	61
Methodist Episcopal	59	"	59
Presbyterian	47	10	57
Baptist	41		41
Jewish	31		31
Unsectarian	31		31
Lutheran	21		21
Reformed (Dutch)	21	4	25
United Presbyterian	7		7
Congregational	6		6
Reformed Presbyterian	5		5
African Methodist Episcopal	6		6
Universalist	5		5
Evangelical	3		3
Unitarian	3		3
Friends	2		2
Reformed Episcopal	2		2
Total Churches			447
Number of Public Schools			121
Total Good Educational Agencies			568

I need only contrast and compare the number of saloons, 10,168, with the number of churches and schools, 568, to show the startling disproportion between agencies for good and evil and speaks in emphatic tones for the increase of the one and the diminution of the other.

The following series of maps with accompanying letter press shows the number of saloons, together with the churches and public schools in each assembly district, and furnishes a strong comment on my previous statement.

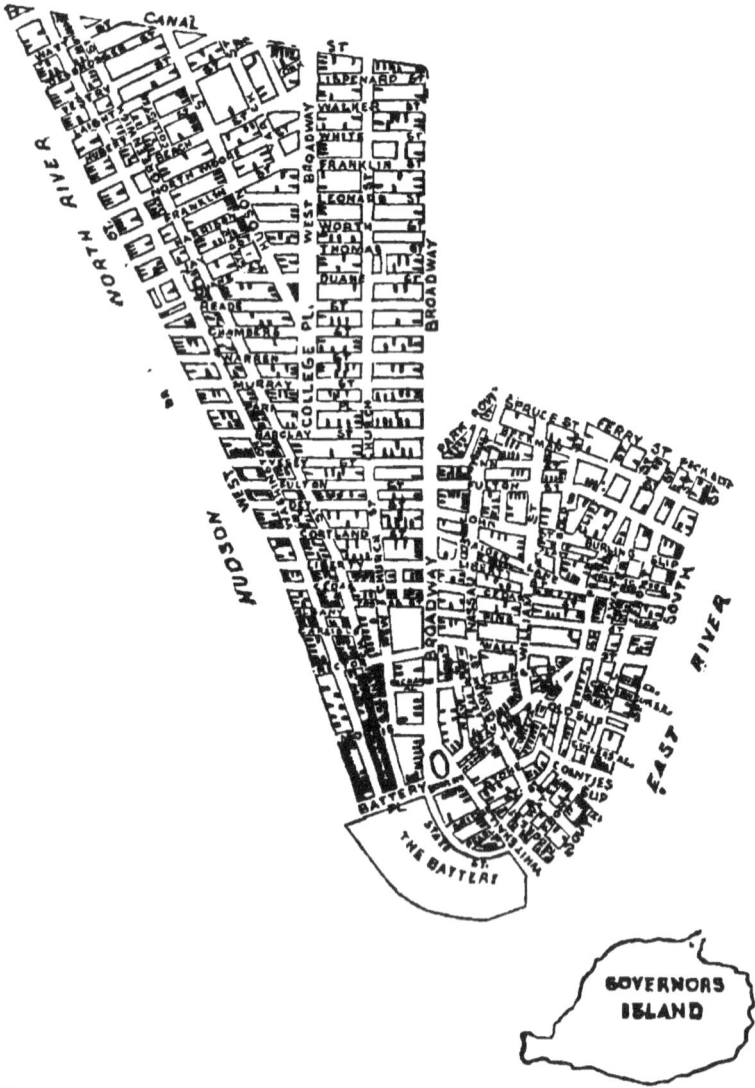

First Assembly District.—Population.......................
Churches, 13 ; Schools, 3............43,998
Saloons (1 to 41 of population)...... 16
1,072

Second Assembly District.—Population.......................47,958
            Churches, 4; Schools, 9..........   13
            Saloons (1 to 94 of population)...   511

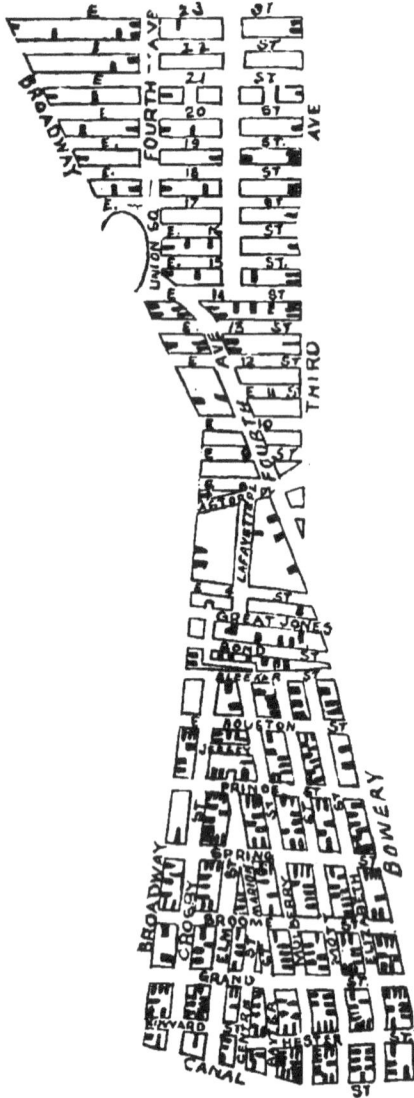

Third Assembly District.—Population........ 49,932
Churches, 14 ; Schools, 5.......... 19
Saloons (1 to 136 of population) :.... 368

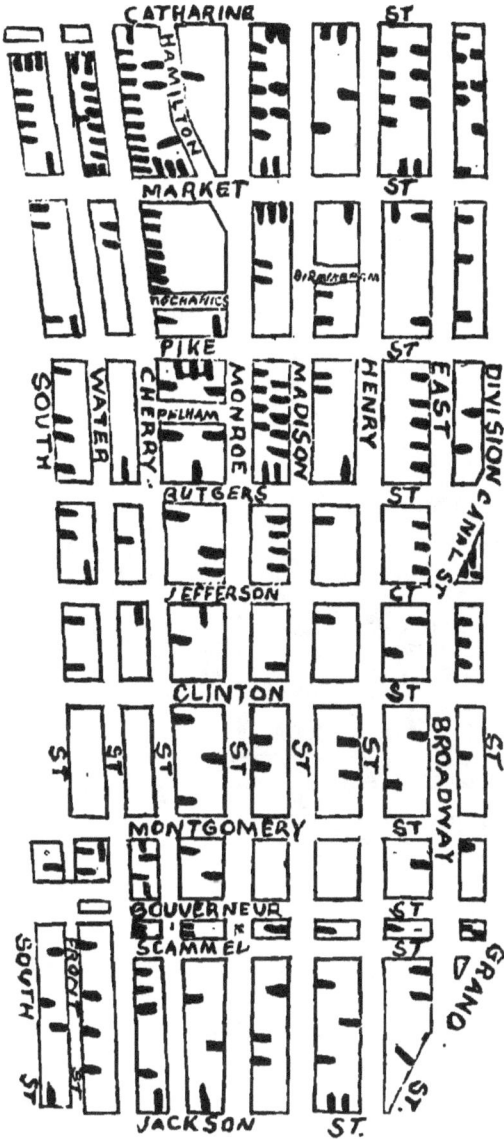

Fourth Assembly District.—Population.......................55,902
Churches, 8 ; Schools, 7.......... 15
Saloons (1 to 275 of population)... 203

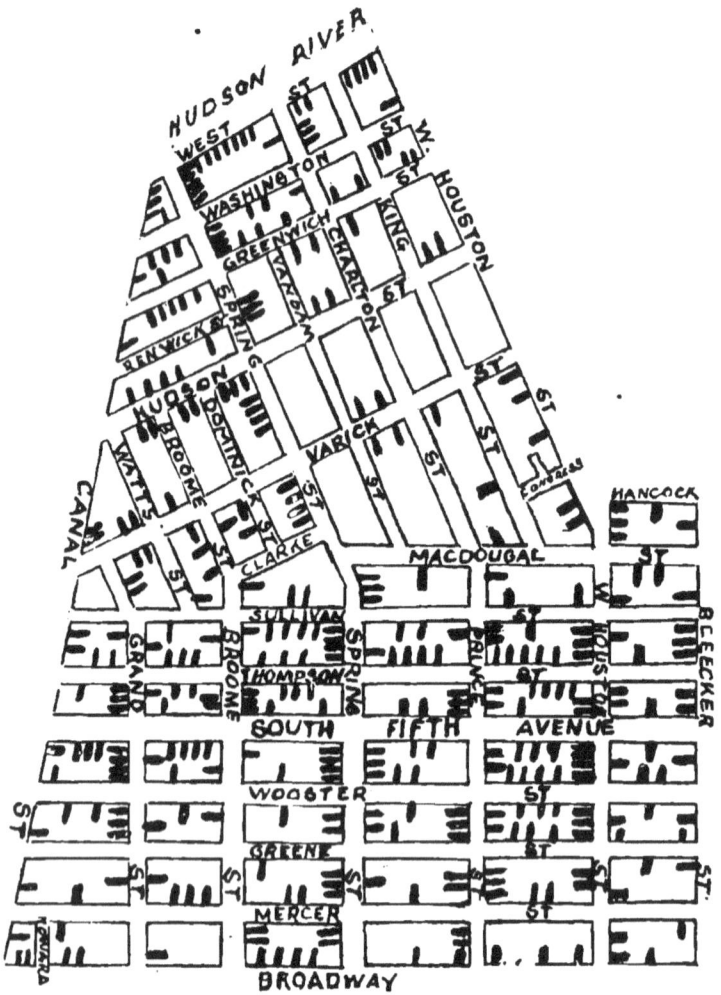

Fifth Assembly District.—Population..........................46,518
                        Churches, 16 ; Schools, 6...........   22
                        Saloons (1 to 147 of population) 315

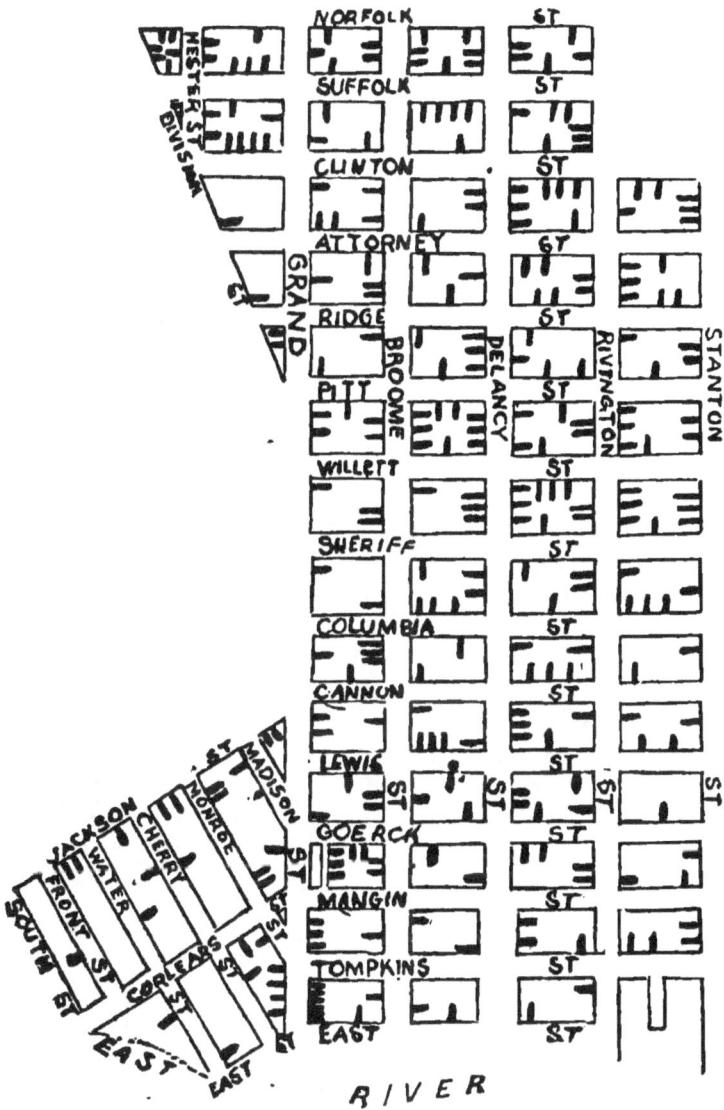

Sixth Assembly District.—Population................. 52,524

Churches, 30; Schools, 3............. 33

Saloons (1 to 182 of population..... 288

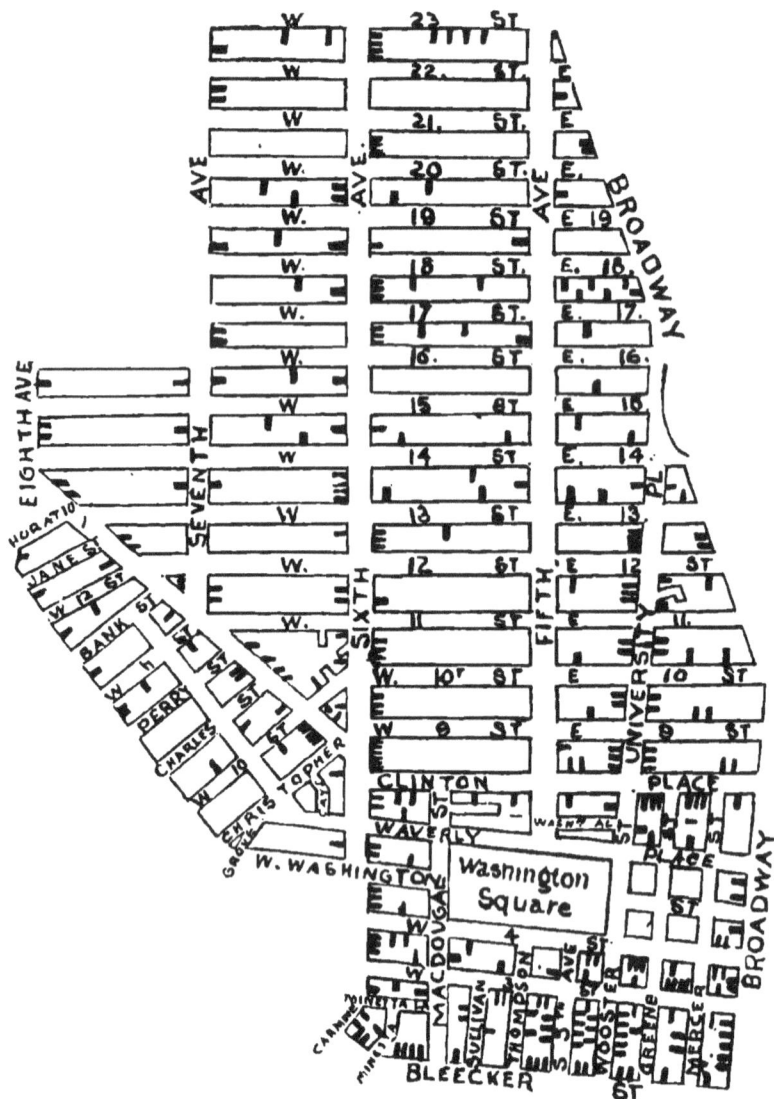

Seventh Assembly District.—Population......................62,406
Churches, 21 ; Schools, 6........ 27
Saloons (1 to 161 of population... 388

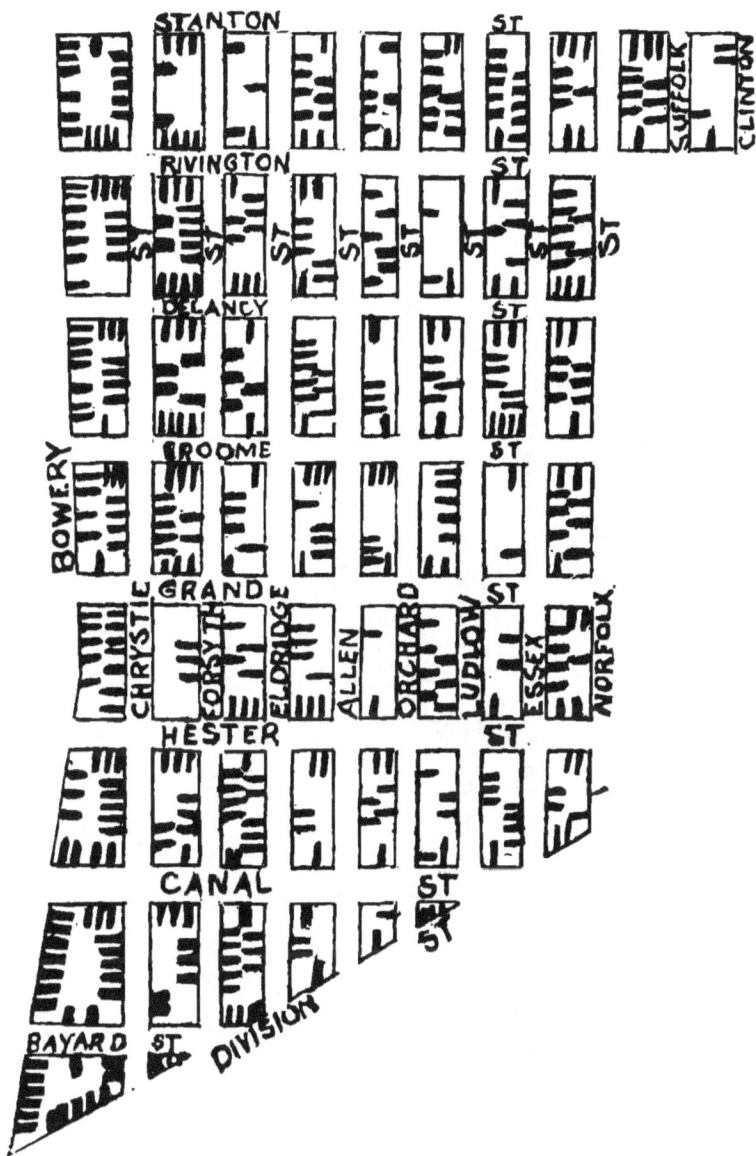

Eighth Assembly District.—Population......................57,342
                    Churches, 12; Schools, 17......... 17
                    Saloons (1 to 119 of population... 482

Ninth Assembly District.—Population........................63,870

Churches, 29 ; Schools, 8........ .   37

Saloons (1 to 228 of population)...   231

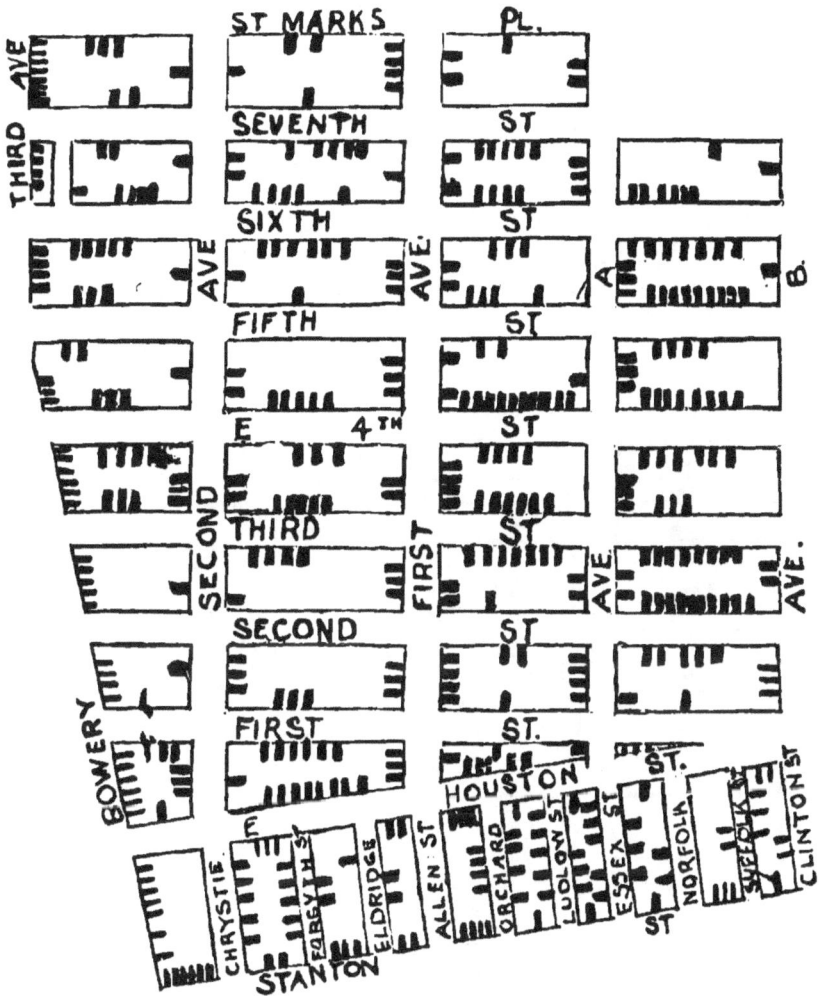

Tenth Assembly District.—Population........................62,196
Churches, 17; Schools, 5.......... 22
Saloons (1 to 169 of population).... 368

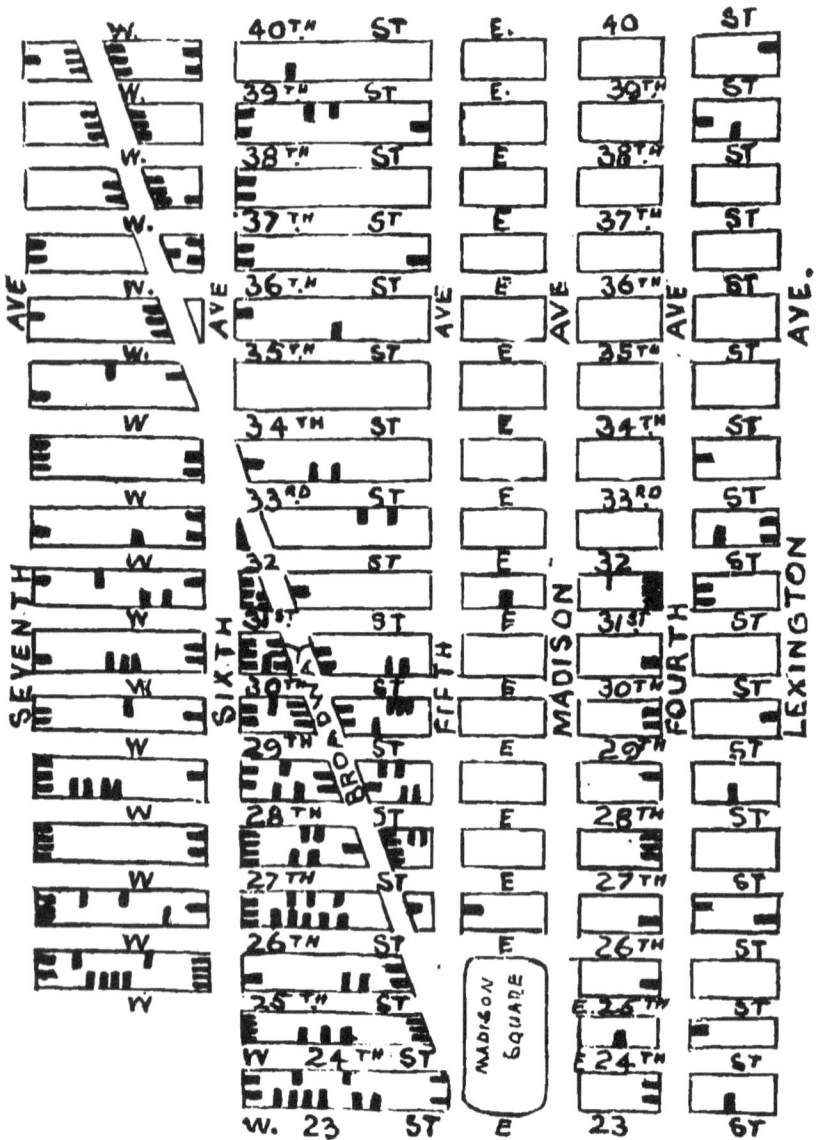

Eleventh Assembly District.—Population.....................45,654

Churches, 16; Schools, 5........ 21

Saloons (1 to 144 of population). 317

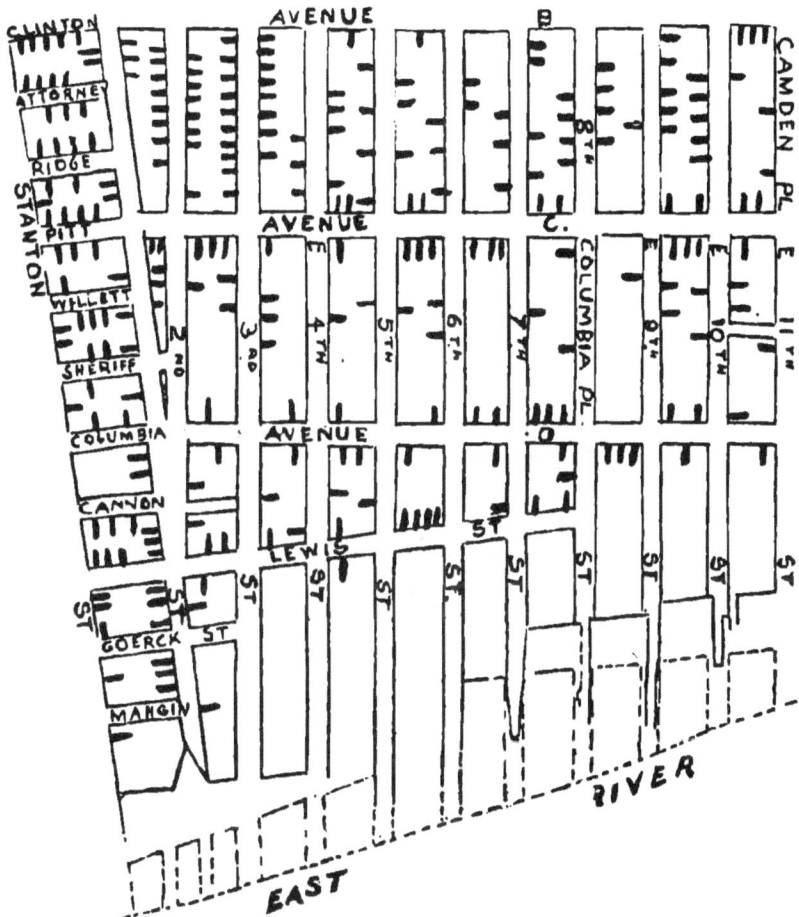

Twelfth Assembly District.—Population.....................51,306
  Churches, 28; Schools 4........ 32
  Saloons (1 to 131 of population). 399

Thirteenth Assembly District.—Population............................60,972
Churches, 25 ; Schools, 1................. 26
Saloons (1 to 259 of population).......... 235

27

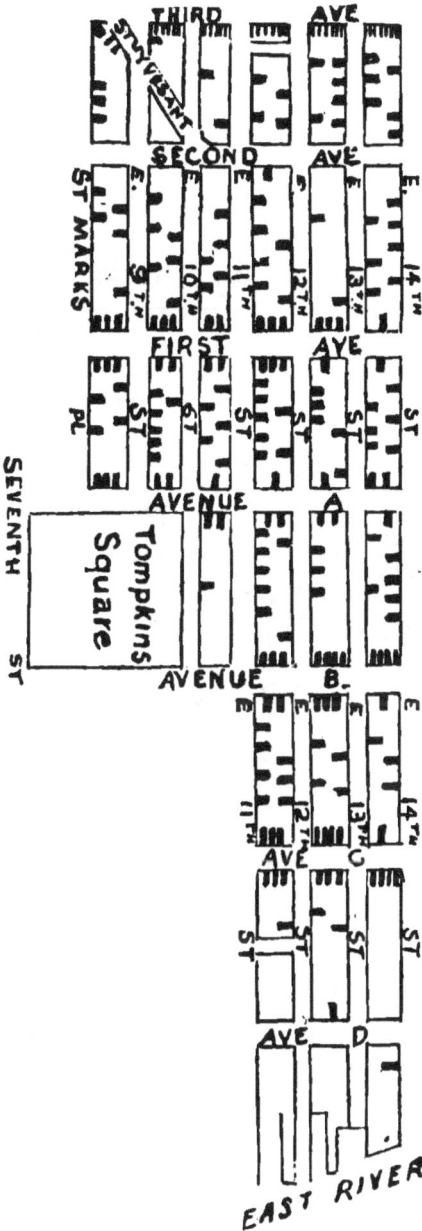

Fourteenth Assembly District.—Population.............................42,216
                         Churches, 19; Schools, 1......   20
                         Saloons (1 to 197 of population)...,..... 214

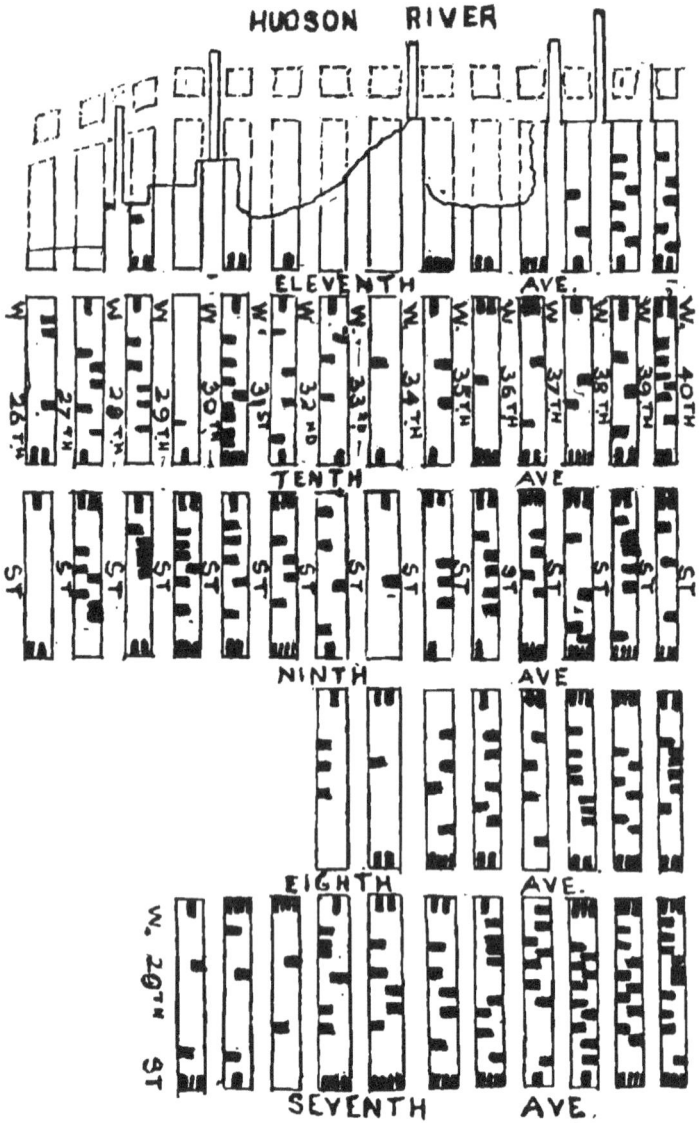

HUDSON RIVER

ELEVENTH AVE.

TENTH AVE.

NINTH AVE.

EIGHTH AVE.

SEVENTH AVE.

Fifteenth Assembly District.—Population.................................69,234

Churches, 28; Schools 1................ 29

Saloons (1 to 148 of population)........... 467

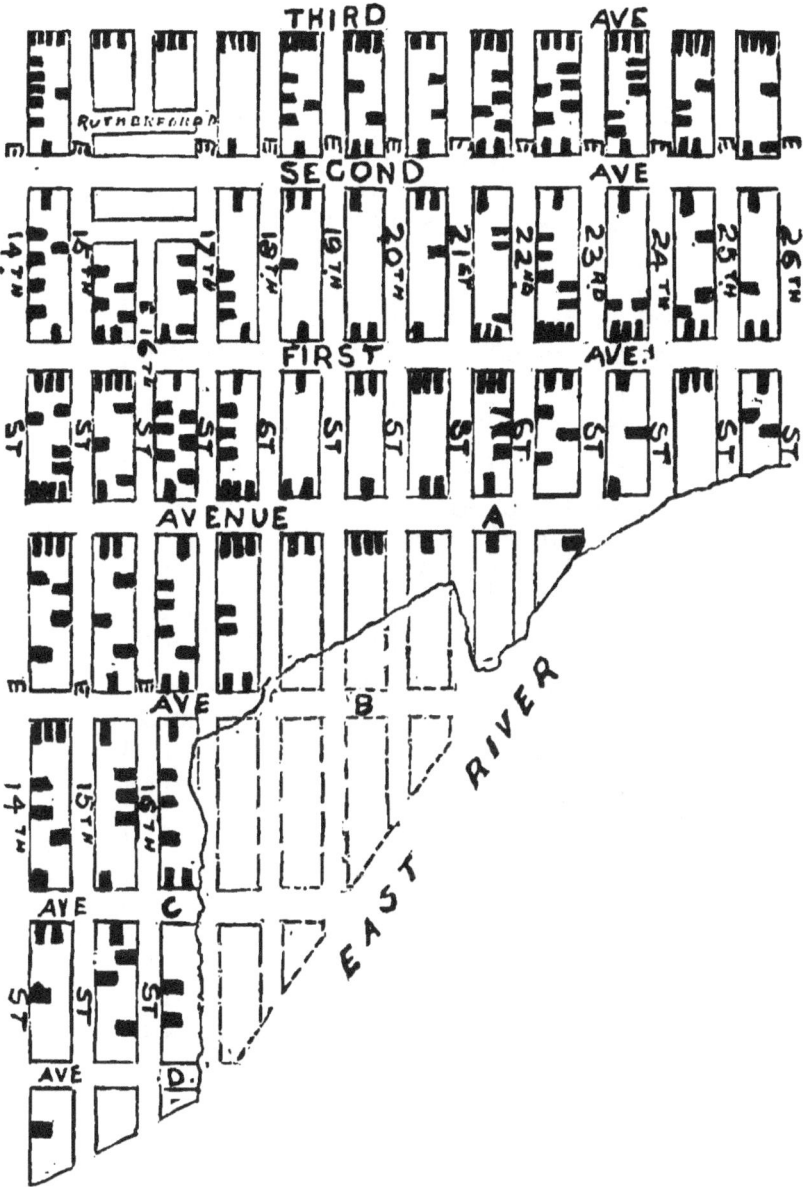

Sixteenth Assembly District.—Population....... 51,879
Churches, 17; Schools, 1.... 18
Saloons (1 to 149 of population).......... 347

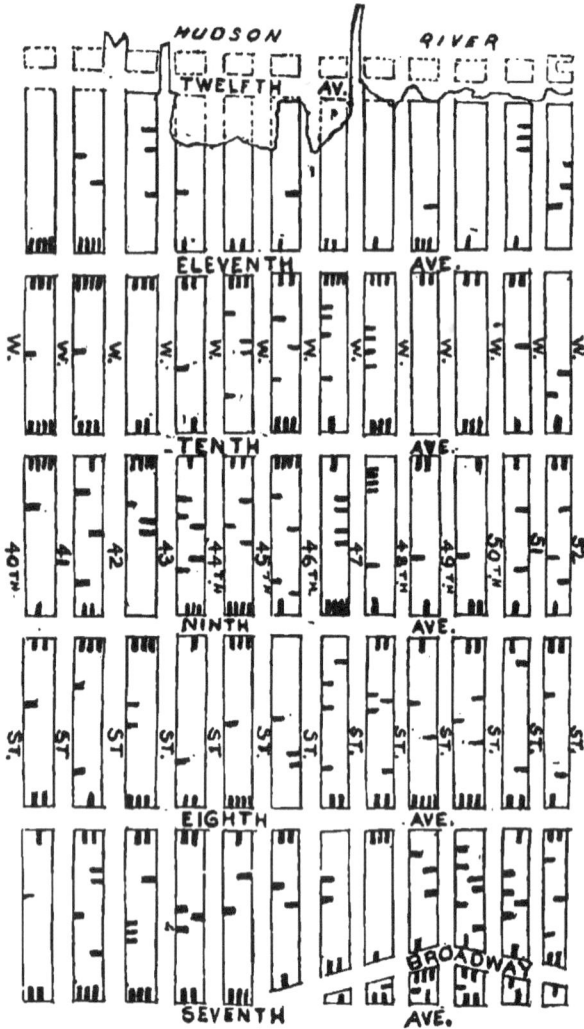

Seventeenth Assembly District.—Population..............................75,036

Churches, 26 ; Schools, 5...............   31

Saloons (1 to 302 of population..........   248

31

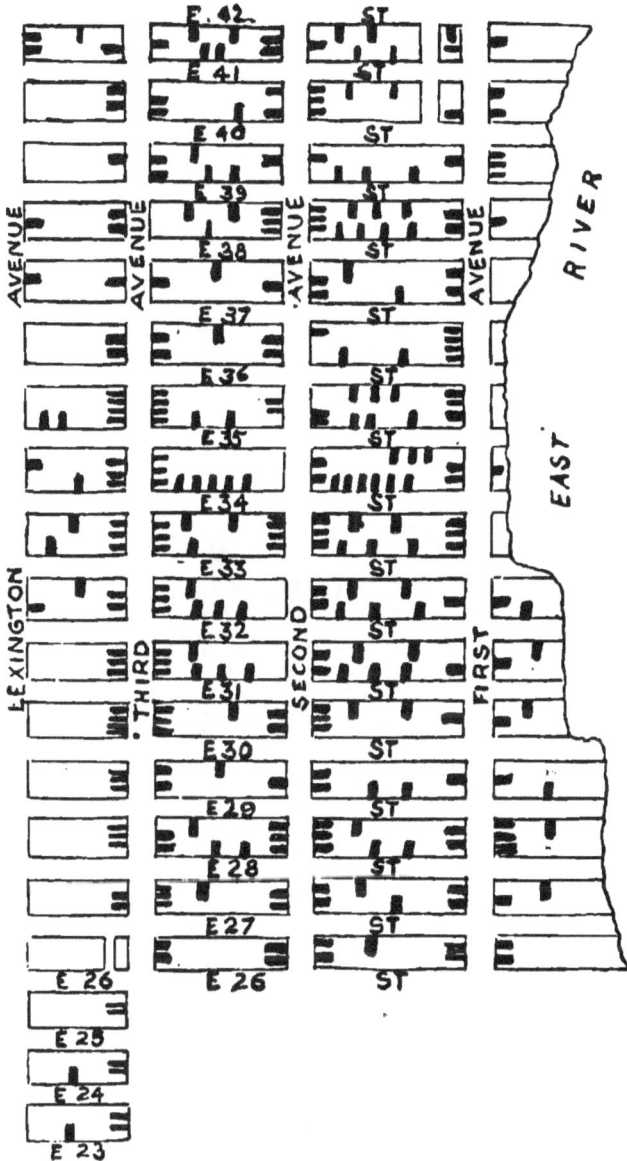

Eighteenth Assembly District.—Population.................................58,824
                      Churches, 26 ; Schools, 10........ 36
                      Saloons (1 to 186 of population).......... 327

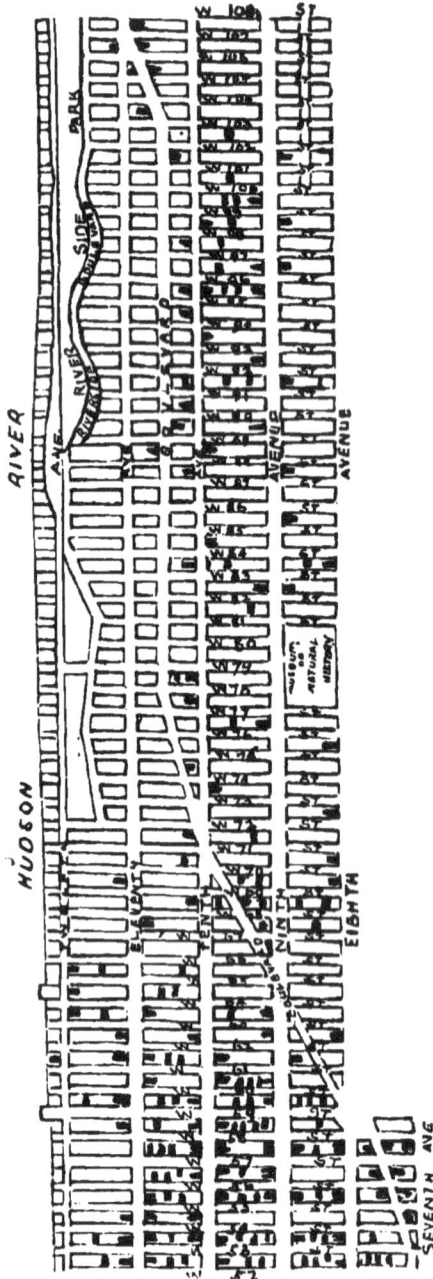

Nineteenth Assembly District.—Population................................72,996

Churches, 39; Schools, 8................ 38

Saloons (1 to 152 of population).......... 480

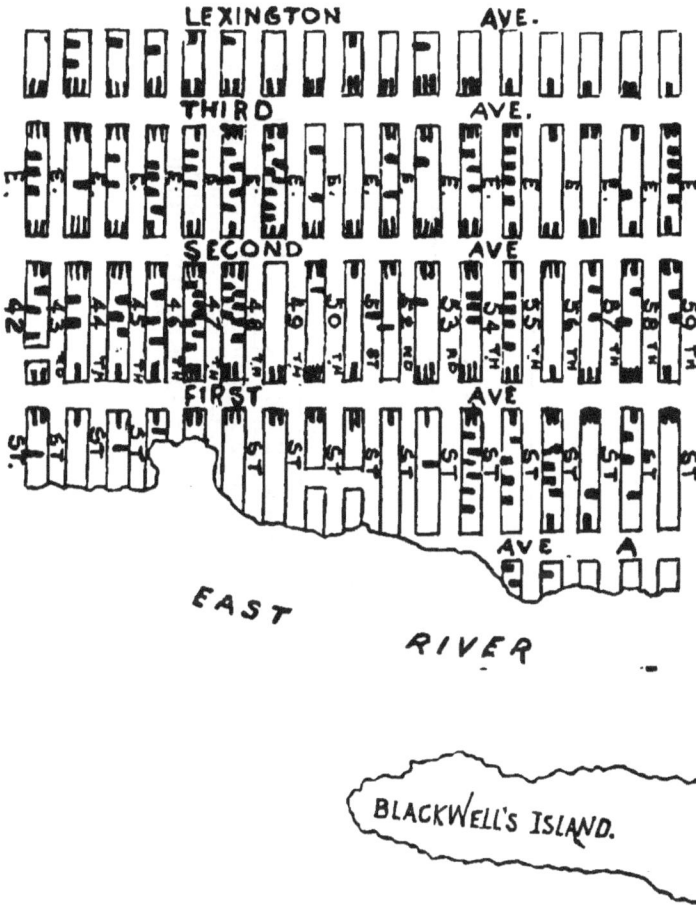

LEXINGTON AVE.

THIRD AVE.

SECOND AVE.

FIRST AVE.

AVE. A

EAST RIVER

BLACKWELL'S ISLAND.

Twentieth Assembly District.—Population..............................60,738

Churches, 7; Schools, 9.................. 16

Saloons (1 to 211 of population).......... 287

84

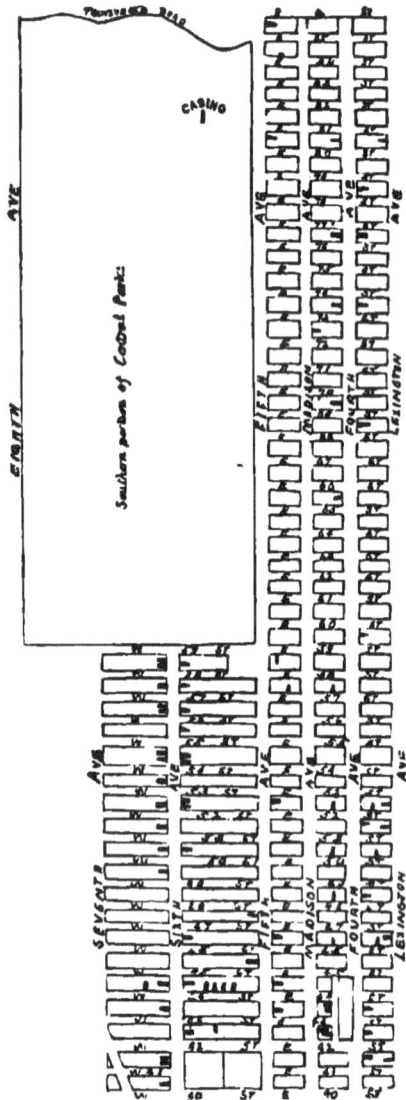

Twenty-first Assembly District.—Population.............................56,748
                           Churches, 9; schools 4................... 13
                           Saloons (1 to 391 of population),,,,,,,,, 145

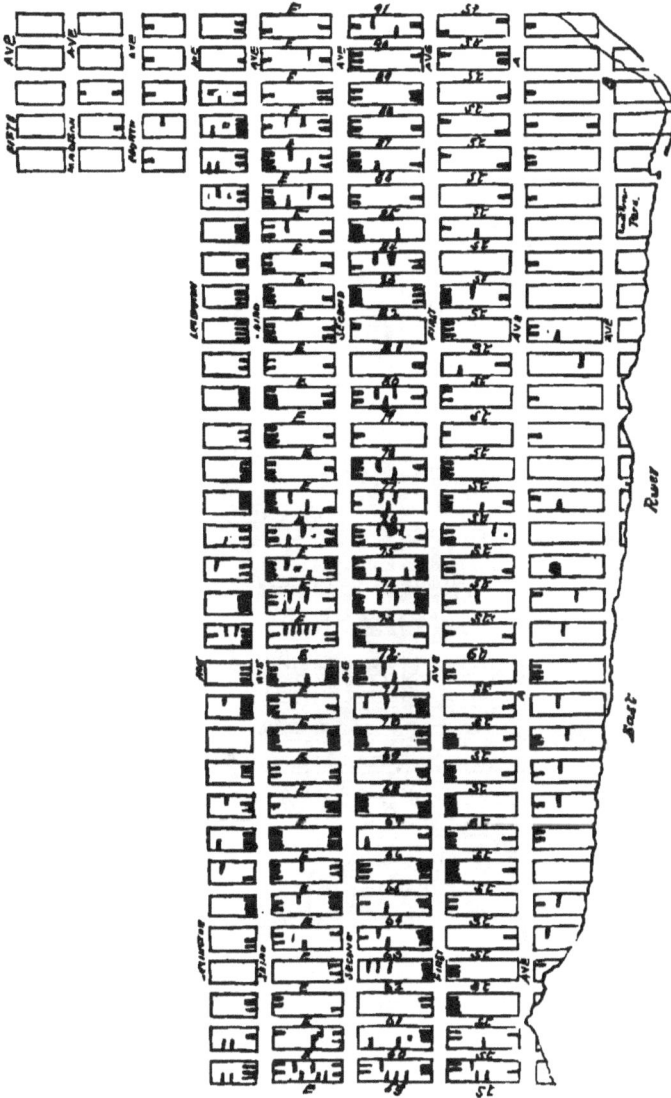

Twenty-second Assembly District.—Population..........................94,302

Churches, 10 ; Schools, 2.............   12

Saloons (1 to 204 of population),......   463

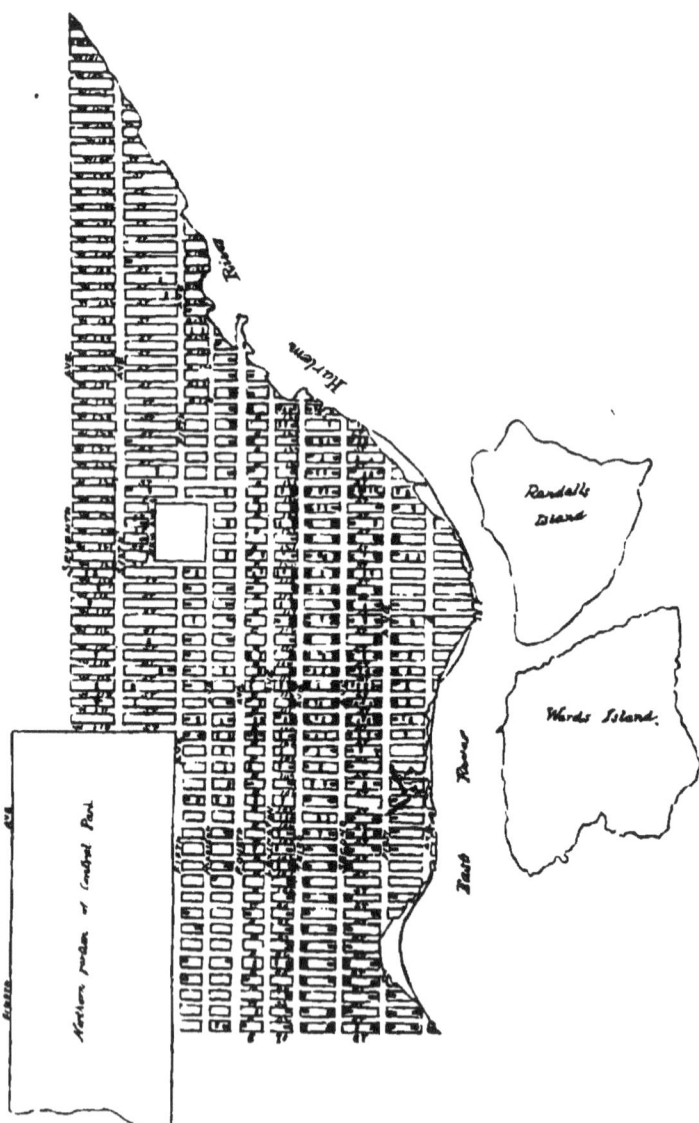

Twenty-third Assembly District.—Population.............................105,048
                                    Churches, 19 ; schools, 3...............   22
                                    Saloons (1 to 179 of population)........ 586

III.

THE SALOON IN MUNICIPAL GOVERNMENT.

IT is one of the cardinal doctrines of our constitution that all men are born free and equal. Our franchise is wider and freer from technical disability than that of any other nation on the globe. This necessitates a keener political intelligence—a readiness to submit to the true law of liberty—an appreciation of the fact that the world's eyes are keenly ˙noting in what measure and to what degree the government of the people, is by the people and for the people—and that because our franchise is wider, it is necessary that our individual political wisdom should be greater.

As is well known, until the late election for Mayor, when considerable disruption of party ties took place, the political control of the city has been in the hands of two principal political parties, viz : Republicans and Democrats.

The latter have been subdivided into sections known as Tammany Hall, Irving Hall and County Democracy.

Each of these organizations has to a greater or less degree fallen into the hands of professional politicians, so disreputable that the term politician has become a hissing and a by-word ; another name for venality and fraud, instead of embodying the highest aspirations of our best citizens.

The instrument most largely used by the class of venal politicians is the saloon. In order that the indictment may be perfectly definite and plain, I submit the following statement of facts obtained by personal investigation into each particular case by a committee of our Calvary Branch, the documents for their verification being in their hands.

Places where primary and convention meetings were held preceding the elections of November, 1884 :

	LIQUOR SALOONS.					NEXT DOOR TO SALOONS.					NEITHER.				
	Tammany Hall.	Irving Hall.	County Democracy.	Republican.	Total.	Tammany Hall.	Irving Hall.	County Democracy.	Republican.	Total.	Tammany Hall.	Irving Hall.	County Democracy.	Republican.	Total.
Congressional Convention....	6	7	6	:	19	:	1	:	:	1	3	:	3	:	6
Assembly Convention.........	17	18	19	9	63	:	3	1	3	7	7	3	4	12	26
Aldermanic Convention......	17	19	19	9	64	:	3	1	3	7	7	2	4	12	25
Primaries.................	16	19	443	9	487	:	3	65	3	71	8	2	204	12	226
Totals.............	56	63	487	27	633	:	10	67	9	86	25	7	215	36	283

Political Meetings held in Saloon 633

Political Meetings held next door to Saloon. 86

                              719

Political Meetings held apart from Saloons.. 283

               Total........ 1,002

It is no part of the object of this pamphlet to discriminate between political parties, but granted government by party, that each should come before its constituency with clean hands, to be judged fairly on its merits, and to stand or fall by the personal honor of their candidates, the purity of their record and the honesty and ability with which their platform has been advocated and their principles carried out.

The inferences to be drawn from the schedule are plainly that the saloon is master of the position : that the saloon-keepers are the political wire-pullers ; that politicians, in the best sense of the term, do not care to submit to the thraldom involved in hobnobbing with keepers of corner groggeries ; and that we have, therefore, the worst and not the best stratum from which to draw our municipal counsellors and State legistors.

THE BOARD OF ALDERMEN.

Three years ago when I made my first cursory investigation into the liquordom of New York city, the twenty-four City Fathers consisted of twelve saloon or ex-saloon keepers ; four professional politicians and eight engaged in other occupations. Of the Board of 1885, it is a matter of common notoriety that two are in Sing Sing, a third is ready to take his place there ; two are in Canada and two in Europe for their health's sake, the air of New York not suiting their constitutions ; three are common approvers, and the balance with three exceptions are awaiting in fear and anxiety the day when they shall take their position before Judge Barrett for the honor of a striped suit, and free but not luxurious maintenance at the cost of the State of New York.

Up to 1884 the Board thus constituted had the confirming power in the appointment of three Excise Commissioners. How that power was exercised may be readily imagined. The Excise Board was a means of sustaining and extending the trade to which they owed their political existence.

Clearly the first step in reform was to take away the confirming power from a body of men, a majority of whom were liquor dealers of the third class. Law is only valuable when there is behind it an honest enforcing power. Thanks to the vigor and energy of Theodore Roosevelt, an act was passed taking away the confirming power of the Board of Aldermen, and concentrating the responsibility in the hands of the Mayor. That power was exercised for the first time by Mayor Grace in 1886. When waited upon by a deputation of the Church Temperance Society, he promised to appoint men for fitness and not for partisan political services.

That promise has been honestly kept, and we have to-day a Board of Excise who, in the interests of the people and in the face of fierce opposition, have taken the first steps towards rescuing the city from the thraldom of its masters—the liquor dealers.

THE BOARD OF EXCISE.

ONE of my first experiences with the Excise Commissioners of New York was when, in 1883, I was one of a deputation appointed to put certain unpleasant questions to that body touching the character of certain well known liquor sellers, named Billy McGlory, Shang Draper, The Allen, Owney Geoghegan, Tom Gould and others.

Their knowledge of law was small, their sense of right—dim ; and their sympathy was evidently with the law-breakers.

An honest Board of Excise must expect obloquy and vituperation. Their duties are difficult ; the law under which they act is confused and contradictory—they beard men whose arm is far reaching, and who largely control political councils.

It is therefore refreshing to read the following preamble and resolutions as the unanimous statement of Messrs. Woodman, Andrews and Van Glahn, the present Board of Excise Commissioners.

Whereas, there are about 9,000 places licensed in this city for the sale of intoxicating liquors ; and

Whereas, this state of affairs is wholly inconsistent with a high degree of public morality and safety, but is directly conducive to poverty, wickedness and crime ; and

Whereas, despite the stringent rules adopted by this Board regarding the opening of new places, and despite our persistent refusal to grant such licenses, save where there is a clearly defined need, the pressure upon the Commissioners to increase the number of drinking places is increasing and well nigh intolerable ; and

Whereas, it is undisputed that the majority of the inmates of Charitable Institutions receiving, by law, the excise monies, are brought there directly or indirectly as the result of intemperance, therefore

Resolved, that in order to promote temperance, and to increase the revenues from which the poor and unfortunate in our institutions are largely supported, the grades of licenses and the fees therefor be and hereby are fixed as follows :

License to sell strong and spirituous liquors, wines, ales and beer, to be drank on the premises............	$200.00
License to sell ale, beer and wines only, to be drunk on the premises......................	$50.00
License to sell ale and beer only, to be drank on the premises...	$30.00

Resolved, that the grades and fees here established shall apply to all licenses issued on or after the 15th day of February, 1887.

The Excise Law left a discretionary power in the hands of the Excise Commissioners to charge as license fee for saloons from $75 to $250. Under previous Boards that discretion was uniformly held to mean the lowest fee of $75, and which was accordingly the fee paid by the retail liquor trade in general and the Board of Aldermen in particular. The law was discriminated in their favor. Now they must pay as the law directs and the city gets the first limited instalment of High License.

A second and much more searching measure is now under consideration of the Board—viz. that of granting in no Assembly District licenses beyond the limit of one to every five hundred of the population.

If adopted, (and the law clearly gives the Board this power) it will reduce the number of saloons from 9,000 to 2,500. This result will not come promptly but it will come inevitably, and the men who are brave enough to face and to force on this issue, deserve the thanks and the support of the community for reducing as fast and as far as the law will allow, this octopus of city life to such modest and manageable dimensions.

Whether the Excise Board may not take the initiative in prosecuting those who have lived under the easy rule of the past—have broken the law—found bail, straw or otherwise—and then deliberately repeated the offence, we may safely leave to the judgment and discretion of the men who have so far deserved well of the city.

THE POLICE COMMISSIONERS.

In a large body like the Police of the City of New York, it is impossible but that there should be some black sheep. It is well, also, to remember that the keenest wits of law breakers are always at work to outwit the law and its guardians. The law against sale of liquors on Sundays to minors, and to intoxicated persons, is notoriously and flagrantly broken.

I do not say that is always the fault of the police—arrests are made in large numbers, but convictions don't follow—why—to be hereafter considered.

It is no part of my object to consider the advantage in directness and efficiency of a single head of the Police Board over the present divided authority—no part of my object to consider the rumors and insinuations against certain police captains who are supposed to know more about disreputable houses, gambling dens, and places where liquor is illegally sold than they acknowledge.

Pressure of public opinion can only be brought to bear for increase of arrests when conviction is reasonably certain to follow a well laid and proved indictment.

THE DISTRICT ATTORNEY.

When I, with others, waited on the Hon. John McKeon, the then District Attorney, in relation to the reputed large number of liquor cases in the pigeon holes in his office, we were informed that there were 9,000 liquor cases, hung up pending settlement. Why? because the office must deal with cases involving liberty first, and there were neither staff nor courts enough to try the cases promptly.

The contention may be made stronger in the case of its

present occupant, Mr. Martine, whose hands have been fairly and fully occupied with the boodle Aldermen.

Nothing is of greater importance to the quietude and well being of the city, than the active and prompt administration of justice. In the case of New York it is known and acknowledged that one whole section of misdemeanants break the law—give bail which is never called up; promptly repeat the offence and thus laugh at law and justice.

What is needed to remedy the evil? Only an additional court room for the third judge, who has now no local habitation and is therefore compelled with his brethren to take his annual vacation of five months.

What would be thought of the head of a dry goods house who provided three high salaried and capable heads of departments, and then condemned them to inactivity one-third of the year.

There is every reason to suppose that if the additional court room was granted the dangerous laxity prevailing would disappear.

Prompt and certain justice, whether for the Hoffman House or Billy McGlory would be an admirable solvent, and give vigor, directness and efficiency to the Excise and Police Departments, with which it is imperative that there be cordial, coöperation on the part of the District Attorney's office.

HIGH LICENSE BILL.

THERE are two possible legislative remedies to be applied to the liquor evil in the City of New York : Prohibition and Restriction.

I do not propose here to touch the justice of Prohibition, only its expediency for large cities like New York. The first factor is public sentiment and opinion. At the last election for the Mayorality the votes were as follows :

Hewitt	90,512
George	68,110
Roosevelt	60,435
Wardwell	582
	219,992

Wardwell was the nominee of the third party Prohibition-ists. He polled one to 186 as against Hewitt; one to 117 as against George; one to 104 as against Roosevelt, one 378th of the whole vote.

That the 582 should lay down the law and enforce it on the 219,992 is the sublimity of audacity.

The bulk of the 219,000 object to butt at the windmill like Sancho Panza—and they look for another remedy. Failing in the conversion of the community to total abstinence, they would like to limit and restrict in accordance with public opinions. The Church Temperance Society endeavored first to master the preliminary conditions of the problem in "Liquordom." Second : The improvement and simplification of the enforcing authority in Mayor, Aldermen, Excise and Police Commissioners and District Attorney. Third : Improvement and codification of the law.

That law was passed in 1837, '67, '70 and '73, and because we have no parliamentary draughtsman to draw these acts and amendments the result was obscure and confusing.

Three gentlemen, experts and lawyers of good standing from the Church Temperance Society and the Society for the Prevention of Crime, drew a complete Bill for the whole State, retaining what was good in the old law, and adding the following :

1. A broad distinction between distilled and fermented liquors, the license fee for the former being $1,000, for the latter $100.
2. Disqualifying convicts from holding licenses.
3 The disqualification of premises for one year, on conviction or revocation of license.
4. The publication of name and address of applicant at least one week before a license is granted.
5. Prohibiting the sale of liquors to minors, under penalty of revocation of license.
6. Prohibiting sale of liquor on board excursion boats and in tenement houses.
7. Requiring licensees to keep the interior of their premises open to view.
8. Care has been taken that no provision of this Bill shall infringe upon or affect the "Civil Damage Act," or the " Local Option Law."

That Bill was our contribution to the Temperance Legislation of the future. It hurt and antagonized the trade ; and it dealt too little in Utopia to suit the third party. No liquor, and controlling liquor power, therefore, combined against it, and it did not become a law.

This year we present a simple amendment to the amended law of 1857.

In cities containing three hundred thousand inhabitants, and more, licenses shall be of the following six classes :

1. Liquor License—To sell liquors of any kind to be drunk on the premises.

2. Wine and Beer License—To sell malt liquors, cider and wine, to be drunk on the premises.

3. Beer License—To sell malt liquors and cider to be drunk on the premises.

4. Storekeeper's Liquor License—To sell liquors of any kind not to be drunk on the premises.

5. Storekeeper's Beer License—To sell malt liquors, cider and wine, not to be drunk on the premises.

6. Druggist's License—Licenses to druggists and apothecaries to sell liquors of any kind for medicinal, mechanical and chemical purposes only, to such persons only, as may certify in writing for what use they want it. The fees for such last mentioned licenses shall be as follows :

For a license of the first class, not less than $1,000.00.

For a license of the second class, not less than $250.00.

For a license of the third class, not less than $100.00.

For a license of the fourth class, not less than $100.00.

For a license of the fifth class, not less than $25.00.

For a license of the sixth class, not less than $100.00.

The Bill is now before the Legislature, introduced by the Hon. E. H. Crosby. It meets the fierce opposition of the doctrinaires who denounce license as a sin, and would therefore condemn New York to the undisturbed and uncontrolled power of Liquordom. The liquo rtrade oppose it because they know that it will wipe out three-fourths of their number.

We desire for High License that it will do two things :

1. It will largely diminish the number of saloons, and therefore the temptation arising from them.

2. It will compel those remaining to pay a tax proportionate to the mischief they do.

It will not bring the Milennium but it will reduce the saloons to a measurable and manageable quantity.

COFFEE TAVERNS.

THE liquor saloon meets one want and makes another. It meets the want of warmth, freedom and company. It makes want, poverty and crime. If it be necessary to largely diminish the number of saloons because of the misery which flows from them, it is equally necesary to provide places of innocent recreation and amusement:

> "Saloons without the drink
> Where men may sit and read and think."

The need of such places in a population so crowded as New York is obvious, the question is, how can they be provided without any taint of charity, and on such practical business basis as shall insure their permanence.

A committee is now engaged in investigating what number and class of lodging houses exist for providing respectable accommodation for young men at a cheap rate. 2nd. What number of cheap restaurants are established. 3rd. What would be the cost of starting on or near the Bowery a place which should combine the restaurant, the lodging-house, together with smoking-room, games-room, and entertainment or lecture hall.

This can best be done by a Limited Liability Company, not intended to pay a large dividend, but to make a fair return on the investment.

The Committee propose to draw their conclusions purely from an investigation into the special conditions of population in New York.

If in this pamphlet I have succeeded in making my meaning plain, I have emphasized the point that true temperance reformation in this city must be carried forward concurrently on these lines:

1st. *The promotion of temperance* by an accurate knowledge of the facts of the case and the evils that spring from intemperance.

2nd. *The reformation of the intemperate*, by persistent, sympathetic action, and personal rescue work on the part of the individual.

3rd. *The removal of the cause of intemperance*, by a stringent, restrictive license law, which shall diminish the temptation offered by the ubiquitous liquor saloon.

www.ingramcontent.com/pod-product-compliance
Lightning Source LLC
Chambersburg PA
CBHW021557270326
41931CB00009B/1264